the year our grandmothers died

Michaela Godding

AOS Publishing, 2025

Copyright © 2025

Michaela Godding

All rights reserved under International and
Pan-American copyright conventions

ISBN: 978-1-83432-001-4

Cover Design: Meredith Lindsay

Visit AOS Publishing's website:
www.aospublishing.com

For Bobby—

who was my best friend, my grandmother, my home and now my angel,

For Rose Marie—

who was and is all of the same to my partner Louay,

and for the extra grandmother that he and I each gained through bridging our families.

Table of Contents

before 1

playing god 3
David's Rabbits 4
deluge 5
Ode to Hot Dogs 6
gone fishing 11
after Aunt Joan died 12
my greatest fear 13
nature's law 15
the truth is that 18
Choosing Goodbye 19

after 21

noise 23
grief cleaning 24
when the bed is an open wound that you can't stop tending to 25
relapse 26
the truth 27
lib·er·ty 28
Cala 30
and it won't be hard to find You still 31
Robertson Clan 32
I pray often 34
someone's favorite story... 35
happily ever 38
glass half 39

before

playing god

(The average person forgets ninety percent of their dreams. I have started keeping tallies on a notepad next to my bed to keep track of all the forgetting. I wonder if endings are all we can rely on. I wonder and wonder and remember that eighty percent of the human body's heat comes out from the head and I wonder if wondering will burn me to pieces.)

They say that life is easier when you are younger, that you can breathe and swallow at the same time until you are seven months old, that as a four-year-old you ask approximately four hundred and fifty questions a day. They say that what you can't control you should put in god's hands. My hands have twenty-seven bones, twenty-nine joints and at least one hundred and twenty-three other named ligaments but I wonder. I wonder about the unnamed ones. I wonder about the fifty thousand cells that will die and be replaced in your body by the time you finish reading this sentence.

David's Rabbits

He insisted on buying the twenty-seven rabbits, confident that a fence would keep the wilderness away from the mass of them in the front yard. despite everyone reminding him of his torn-to-bits trash cans from the ever growing sleuth of New England black bears, He was sure that the small quiet creatures would survive the elements that they were born to live in. my Grandmother, his wife, had grown too old to nod her head   no   anymore, and instead sighed and shrugged as he grunted the metal caging into the still wet grass after arriving with them in the back of his new black truck. I never got to see the rabbits, during the few days they lasted, but my Grandmother swears that they were the purest, sweetest things she had ever laid her eyes on.

deluge

in the years before I knew
what hair dye was, church was an empty
backyard in Colebrook. i never considered
myself rich growing up, but i also didn't know
the difference then between frogs and salamanders;
gods and parents; food and love. the trees didn't mock me
for being fat. instead, we shared breath as stubborn dew slowly wet
my sneakers a green musk. we would all know if there had been more storm
than sun when the yard flooded, the black bears disinterested in the temporary bog
of a property. i guess i just saw myself as more of a newt than a bear. i've always loved the rain.
i even think i saw a hummingbird out there once, but it's hard to know if that is a hope or a memory.

Ode to Hot Dogs

It's funny that I can remember hundreds of car rides, but never the car they take place in.

I do remember that the view from the back seat of my Aunt Patty's car was some sort of dangling gem from her rearview mirror, angrily heaving back and forth as my aunt and cousin yelled at each other about god knows what. I wasn't able to make out the quick appearances of words between the yelled *FUCK*s and Nelly playing through the car's blown out speakers.

As they fought over which exit to take, I watched the highway wind drag raindrops across the backseat passenger window. I imagined the droplets screaming, holding on for dear life, which made me laugh. Ashley turned around to find out what was so funny. I shrugged, keeping my eyes on the window, the greyness outside seeming more vast than usual.

"You're so fucking weird," Ashley snapped before whipping back to the fuckfuckfucks with her mom.

Yelling had always been their way of communicating.

At every family gathering at my grandmother's house, like clockwork, one or both of them would explode, and then retreat to smoke a cigarette on the deck. Minutes later after simmering, they would come right back in, grab a beer and belly laugh as if the yelling had never happened. We were all used to this since their red faces would usually be over
    cupcakes forgotten at home   a broken cup shared shoes that got dirty in the mud.

Despite them both being hotheads, even *they* knew that their qualms wouldn't matter come the next day.

"We're almost theerrreee!" my aunt sing-songed as we pulled off the highway. At that moment, I realized I was nervous.

In my eight-year-old brain it felt strange to be nervous to see my mom, since after all, she was the first person I ever knew. I fiddled with the skirt that I was wearing, a jean mini skirt with green sequined fabric falling to my ankles, a true early 2000's gem. I hated wearing skirts because it meant that I had to focus on keeping my legs shut everywhere I went, and that was hardly at the top of my list of things worth paying attention to. My fiddling then moved up to my matching green shirt

that hid beneath it my discomfort—
the first bra I had ever worn, an ironically matching green one. Bringing my attention to it somehow made the band around me feel even more tight. I hated how it felt, but my aunt talked up how proud my mom would be of me for wearing it.

The previous week my fifth-grade teacher had pulled me aside between classes and whispered that since I was "growing" I needed to get "something to keep it all under wraps".

Despite conveying that I understood, I still refused to wear one, mostly because I knew my dad wouldn't be taking me shopping for one any time soon. My sister had disappeared for what felt like years (and when I look back I see that it actually was years) and my mom had recently become incarcerated, so my boobs being comfortable seemed like the last bit of childlike freedom that I would get to salvage.

When I told my grandmother about Mrs. T's "special request", she did what she always did, and started finding cash from random nooks in her house to give to my aunt and I to plan a shopping trip. One annoying shopping trip to Kmart later, armed with a new bra and a way too sequined skirt, I found myself in the back of my aunt's car heading to York Correctional Facility to visit my mom in prison for the first time without my dad. That moment held too many firsts for my liking, including the nausea I felt from my aunt's rapid stop-and-go braking.

When the car was parked I felt more relieved than nervous since I knew we had made it in one piece. My aunt hustled us inside to make sure that we would make it during visiting hours.
One locker   two pat downs   two security clearance rooms later,
there was my mom waiting with open arms.

We played Uno as my aunt and her caught up, and I sat wondering and wondering if she would notice the new piece of clothing under my shirt since I had last seen her.
Time ticked away as it always would, and when the warden called for visits to be over,
I bitterly   anxiously   helplessly   exclaimed that I was wearing a bra and that my mom hadn't noticed. Before she could respond, I rushed to leave the room with angry-flushed cheeks. Once we got back in the car, the rivers came—

I cried over another moment where what mattered most to me went unseen.

My aunt and cousin reassured me that a bra wasn't the sort of thing that most people can notice since it's hidden under your clothes. To that, I starkly responded that my mom wasn't most people—she was my mom, and that she should know when something is different with her child. My first attempt at showing her that I could grow into myself all by myself had been a complete failure.

I stayed quiet during the drive back to my grandmother's house, which neither my aunt nor cousin minded much as they went back to their song-playing and bickerings.

When we got back around two hours later, my grandmother was cooking something that smelled amazing. Her kitchen was always a joyful clutter of cow knick knacks four leaf clovers mismatched plastic containers and mountains of paper plates for every holiday that you can name off the top of your head.

As she waddled between different pans and the microwave, she sang "hell-ooooo" in her quirky accent. Her love instantly began to thaw my eight year old angst, and even with a hard pressing band on my chest, I still couldn't help but smile.

After I was coaxed into mumbling about my disappointment of the visit, everyone helped me take the bra off in the fish themed bathroom, as lifting it off was a two person job. Finally comfortable, I plopped on the couch and was surprised to see my grandmother had brought me a plate with hot dogs and mac and cheese on it, despite me seeing lobster heads and claws popping out of the giant pan in the kitchen. I could never bear to eat them after watching them boil alive, so she had made the alternative just for me.

As most of my family hee-hawed loudly in the next room as they broke the lobsters with butter, my grandmother sat with me in our usual spots on the couch. Even though I knew she loved lobster, she too had a plate of hot dogs and mac and cheese.

gone fishing

the river down the road is overflowing
after the toomuch rain. david unspools
in his recliner. his snore shimmers knick knacks
all the way to the kitchen where empty beer
bottles and red cheeks debate cards.
auntie needs another smoke break. uncle
too. and cousin ashley. and her boyfriend.
everyone sits cold on the porch blanket couches
with their tiny mouth fires. their grey huffs outside
give good faith that the pies will stay cold on the deck.
when nighttime slaps the sky black, everyone huddles
back in with drunken laughter and kicked off boots.
for a second, home becomes where the fish got caught.

after Aunt Joan died

the pool has had a tarp over it
for six years in a row

the cicadas refuse to stop
mourning even if dead

grass is the easiest to uproot
the cabin is surrounded

by lightning bugs or maybe breaking
stars   (have you ever been face down

in a pond and wondered if drowning
is only for girls that are both beautiful

and patient) my grandmother's
cigarettes dampen the deck wood

as the sun gives up
as it does every day

the frogs erupt in democracy
at the smell of nighttime

my nostrils submerge and I wait
for what isn't coming.

my greatest fear

has always been spiders	has always been dying
the way that it creeps	
into the shadows of basements	into the background noise
and unused tennis racquets	of every family photo
teeth ready	
regardless if it's venom	to break into Christmas
can overcome a creature's	morning with a car crash
smallness	
it will keep biting	has no bible in a house
what threatens it	where people eat
until it makes them sick	
I understand that I'm afraid	the playset I used to
of the creatures' only way of surviving:	piss myself on is now
covered in	
camouflage a spider is meant to	years of my father
seem like something it isn't—as it's	wishing I was a boy
hiding in plain sight	
it never wastes its hereness	has become
contemplating death	one of my greatest hobbies
but	
instead, lives it life opening	if a tree dies in the forest
and reopening its mouth shamelessly	and nobody sees it
science says	
spiders can fly,	it's still dead,
that they can even cross	just unmourned.
entire	
oceans on their	worlds begin and end
silk threads by	every day, red symphonies
ballooning	
them through strong	into blood clots,
wind currents, only	all it takes is one
fall	
-ing back to earth	down the stairs,
by undoing their own	and twelve
bouquets	
of web—god decided	later my memory
you need eight legs to hear the	becomes a thing of the
ionosphere	
: spiders can feel	rusting unreachable static,
the global electric field since	no pulse,
the sun	
's pulsing can be detected by	an unknown warmth
their sensory hairs.	to a greying corpse.

                          this makes me think that some questions
are better unanswered   are better left
like   unasked like
                                    why
can a spider decipher   be born at all
what a human cannot?   if we are meant for devastation?
                              some truths
can't possibly offer   aren't meant to be
the certainty of mother nature   easily swallowed
                                because
if we could ask a spider   maybe we are meant instead
if it has ever experienced   to savor the things we slaughter
                                 regret
maybe, it would say   is a dress best worn
it hates the   by a full and still filling
                                  name
arachnid, and maybe   and I am brimming.
even the spider wishes it   it's true I
                      never knew the ionosphere—
then at least   I never danced among stars,
it could be in only one   I tried accepting that the
                                  place
at one time.   where I'm found dead someday
because   will be a kitchen floor. I
                                   even
spiders have hearts,   started writing my suicide
and even things that   notes in cursive—I know this may
                                 terrify
me are deserving   you, but please know that all
of a   I've ever looked for is a
                                  home.

nature's law

my grandmother is the most Irish of us
both literally and spiritually

her swagger best comes from her
larger-than-life two-honk laugh

even as her years start to bicker
more with her bones

she still manages to down
a whole pack a day

today is the tenth or twelfth time
that she has fallen in the bathroom

I cry because I know that she hates
that she needs

anything
anyone

as her off-white nursing home bed
threatens to keep eating

at her thirty-pound-lighter
frame

she picks
at her spaghettios dinner

and between bites whispers
that a woman keeps coming
in her room at night
flicking on and off the lights

for no reason
at all

we laugh that at least
she isn't that far gone yet

when she gets back
from the hospital this time

her husband breaks
the bad news:

a black bear left only a puddle of blood
in place of her screaming dog

now alone again
in the woods of her home

she shrugs and sits in her knowing:
well it had to happen at some point.

the truth is that

today I thought someone was going to shoot me in the face
when they walked up to my car window.
it just happened to a friend
last week and I've been extra jumpy since.
the truth is that
my car is a piece of a shit, but that doesn't mean that the shallow
layer that it puts between me and everything on sidewalks
doesn't make me feel invisible to the evermovings of
the world   a closed restaurant   a man sleeping on news paper
an argument with a gun   these are the things
that I don't pay mind to
zipped up in my car.
the truth is that
we all like to believe that we won't be the one to die
in a Wendy's parking lot someday, but
the truth is that
sometimes people shoot other people
just to prove to themself that they can.
the truth is that
today I thought someone was going to shoot me in the face
before considering that I might break my skull open
in the shower   on the corner   while cooking
and that says a lot more
about what I *think* I'll see, when
the truth is that
I'm more afraid of being killed
than of actually dying,
because
the truth is that,
if I died today,
I wouldn't be able to tell you
if it was all worth it.

Choosing Goodbye

when his mom   (calls/cries/caves)
we know   there may be only   minutes

he debates   (hand in mine/who to be/prayer)
asking   (me/himself/god)
if a memory of her   (strong/human/alive)
is more important   than saying goodbye

we rush out of   (the door/doubt/our home)
into my car   and sit silent   the whole
way with only   the buzz   of an empty   radio

when we arrive   we climb   (the stairs/lineage/hesitation)
up   to a quiet   room   where we once
all   (sang/learned/celebrated)

her   body is still   (beautiful/warm/hers)   the sun
(gathers/sighs/shows)   a soft   yelloworange
through her favorite   corner window   painting the

(photographs/machine beeps/quiet)   with proof
that mother nature   is still   (viable/forgiving/here)

he holds her   (hand/heart/spirit)
and wishes   for her   infinite   (heavenly gossip/art museums/pansies/
reruns of jeopardy/cheetah print blankets/kefir/views of Cala/laughter)
and then   heavy   with   (grief/love/what comes next)   he

gives   to her   his last
(nothing/hello/goodbye)

and   I swear   I see
(her/the light/the love we have)

give   it all right back.

after

noise

I have always hated churches
each pew a tooth of god's insatiable mouth

organ loud enough to be
a mother screaming
over her dead child's body

I realize I am the only one mourning
who can also read music
as we stand and cry through "Amazing Grace"

I sing the hymns
I ask god to chew her gently
as sharp breaths fill the room

they are almost loud enough
to make me forget about all this
pretending.

grief cleaning

I begin
with the seven
loads
of dirty laundry

sick
of my sink-chest
piled high
with dishes

flies circling
all the forgotten
uneatens

today
tarot says
death is coming

I laugh because
we all know
it is already here

when the bed is an open wound that you can't stop tending to

healing hurts
worse than dying
when it is all you are
allowed.

relapse

hi! it's me! i'm healthy now, didn't you hear?? aren't you excited? maybe, this is the part where i write a book! or maybe, this is the moment i learn to love hiking! that makes sense. new horizon. family bonding. discount code here! have you ever brushed your teeth? have you ever thought that you saw your old body in the background of a movie? no? that's great news! back when i used to be my own ghost, i would see how far down i could swallow my fist! guess how far i got? just two fingers :) anyways, i'm healthy now, so don't worry, i will never be sad! ever again actually! i will point at the oncoming train and say *wow, that's one crazy locomotive!* instead of getting up and doing something! i've gotta say, it's pretty liberating not caring about anything other than caring. i hear you. i see you. i am you. keep up the good work! hi! it's me! i'm healthy now, aren't you excited? maybe, this is the part where i write a book about how much i love hiking! that makes sense. new horizon. family bonding. have you ever brushed your teeth? no? that's great news! keep up the good work! anyways, i'm healthy now, so i will never be sad! i will point at the oncoming train instead of getting up and doing something! i've gotta say, it's pretty liberating caring now. i see you. i am you. keep up the good work! hi! it's me! i'm healthy, aren't you? maybe, this is a book! or maybe, this makes sense. new horizon. family bonding. have you ever thought you could be my own ghost?

the truth

is that in your face I always saw my father's

eyes looking back at me

as my childhood sipped hot
cocoa under the collection of blankets
in your living room, I still remembered
that I was only warm and there
because he once was, too

I now imagine your son as small
as I was then,
tiny, shaky hands gripping
a porcelain mug before slipping
and dropping into shatters
on your splinterwood floor

your heartlaugh then filling
the cracks between the new broken

promising a mother's unbreakable *I forgive you*
before he could learn the love of apology

it's been ten years since he called me his daughter

my blood tells me that he still hasn't learned.

lib·er·ty

/ˈlibərdē/
noun
> 1. the state of being free within society from repressive rules on one's way of life, actions, or opinions.

the president decides to rename the Gulf of Mexico
as the 'gulf of america' and in that moment I hear
your bones shatter   out of the dirt   clicking into
place   hands sewn back together   by fury
just enough   to reach   for your shotgun
that you threatened to grab   eight years ago
at our simply   blessed   republican thanksgiving
as you yelled that you would   *kill him yourself*
if you have to   as your husband prayed   to the lord
and to trump   with the same cigar   at the head
of the table   you had just broken over   to beg
and still beg   with now dead hands   that we
somehow find   the balls   to still call the devil
the devil.

2. the capability to do as one chooses.

the president   pretends to decide   what I wear
to school   even though we all know
the only choice   is a bullet-proof vest   as he rambles
your bones shatter   out of the dirt   clicking into place
just enough   to reach for my   future
children   to warn them of   their hometown burning
the fields   on fire with   silence   and just past them,
freedom:

an Irish hymn   echoing off of a young girl's
scraped knee   blissful   in the belief that all bleeding
things heal   Grandma,   your laid palms
still pray over me   every night   when I ask
the moon to forgive me   for being who I am

even with broken hands   you remind me
that a wolf isn't a woman   with an opinion,
a wolf is a wolf   and that's what I will continue
to call it.

Cala

He told me a story once
about the time his grandmother
had been told to leave her
ex-husband's old beach house
alone—she had lost it
in the divorce, and any key
to it opening was made sure to be put out of
her reach—so when Summer came,
she left for Cala as always, a new
lover at her side—no wrench in hand,
just the iron weight of being
a woman in the 80s, a pulled back arm,
and a frame small enough to slide through
a newly broken window.

and it won't be hard to find You still

a tall glass of Milk

every Easter basket

how I stack the Plastic Containers

a Love-stained sink

dinner in the Living room

an Unused fireplace

hidden Boxes of cookies

Summer's first grill

Two-for-one socks

the Sound of a page turning

Robertson Clan

Growing up with wide hips, it was hard to fit into anything. I would spend hours in kohls   sears   kmart   trying to find clothes that could cover up the features that coaxed other kids to call me a whale. Once a year though, everyone in our family would put away their differences to dress all the kids in proper attire for the annual Scottish Festival, and for once a year, something beautiful would fit me.

We would each be adorned in intricate crosses of red   black   blue   with a sash   all held together by a stunning gem-covered pin passed down from someone that I would never know but that meant a great deal to my grandmother, Bobby. It was these festivals that taught me patience, with it taking an hour just to get the kilt   shoes   tights   hat   hair   perfectly ready, to then trudge the delicates through the rain in some rented out field from tent to tent, stopping at each to learn about the different clans of Scotland.

I remember one Christmas when my whole family pitched in to get me a violin so that I could learn how to fiddle. My cousin was learning step-dancing, and so naturally it was my job to accompany her. I envied her blonde hair and lighter feet, and during her first step performance I cried because I realized that people only liked watching thin little girls dance. Upon saying this, Bobby yanked me aside, shoved a shortbread cookie into my hand, and huffed for me to stop complaining, because *without the violin, my cousin would have nothing to dance to.*

The next year I showed up ready, carrying around my violin case in the rain for three hours before it was finally my turn to perform in a thirty-person tent. I loved how they clapped and sang. I loved being the center of a universe, a part of something. Afterwards, adults flocked to my side, complimenting my bow technique, music theory knowledge, great energy, and stunning ruby pin. My grandmother, seeing me occupied with praise, snuck away to smoke a cigarette in the tent corner with a smile.

When she was finished, she came back and grabbed my cousin and I to go see a goat-judging competition. Bobby bent down next to me quietly to ask, *now was that so bad?* and I yippeed that I couldn't wait to do it again. She laughed and reassured, *It's because you are a Robertson girl, and Robertsons don't let fear win.*

I pray often

not because
I believe
in god,
but to reiterate
that hope
is a choice.

someone's favorite story

Dear Bobby,

I wish you could've lived

your heart powering the electricity
of all three neighboring towns

another Easter ham puckering
at the foot of the dining room table

pastel eggs arriving in a sweep
of decorations and tiny chocolates

chip dip the center of shrimp and stuffed
mushrooms, the living room wood

sorry with another year
of nothing changing,

the fish bowl again watching
me try on mascara for the first night,

the basement freezer a museum
of icicled fossils, the legendary bones

of chicken nuggets and
welch's cylinders

so sweet and so perfect,

every frozen dinner roll
with an upcoming holiday

to romance it
back to life,

one heart attack or chocolate cake
away from being

the in-between
laughs

that helped me
meet forgiveness

more than divorce ever did,
the adult card games,

the strange looking liquor
that I never got to taste,

or even the collection
of dark blue glass bottles

from places you can't remember
the name of anymore

I wish I could watch the hooks
of the kitchen reopening

the cans of green beans,
a new set of candles

for just one more
singing of happy birthday

the pool open one more summer,
hot with toothless joy and

ice pops and sunburn
and new floaties,

the kept promise that
some places really do stay beautiful

when they are untouched by
humanity and sinning

and love and love and

barbecues and
fire,

the foliage and ashes,
letting

even the smallest of towns
be the beginning

of someone's
favorite story.

happily ever
written after "ALTERNATE ENDING—FOR MY FATHER", by Isabelle Correa

In this version					we return
							to the waterfalls

							the mosquitos don't bite
my leg hairs are long				enough
to shimmer in lake

you are happy					you had a daughter

you teach me about loudness:
how to find it   how to sing it
as the endless rush of nature
pools at our pale white feet

as we cross the rocks together
the river becomes a wedding aisle
your arm there to make sure
I don't fall

I don't

the trees applaud   the water roars
at the matrimony of this

In this version you let					me
go.

glass half

I'm sorry

for this mess all over the all over

the carpet

dragging at my heels
like a half dead dog

look at me

my empty is so big

my stomach full
of stars
unapologizing

on the way down

at least I can say
I bellied the sky.

THANK YOU

Louay, my love, my soulmate, thank you for your bottomless support in me bringing this book to life. You immediately understood the importance of this heart-project, and without a blink helped me make it happen. Thank you for believing in my words, and their ability to respect your experience of losing someone next to my own. I'm so grateful that we had each other through these huge life changes, and I know our grandmothers are incredibly proud of us.

Vicki, thank you for getting married right as my grandmother's health began to drastically decline. Fate made sure I would be at your side as you got ready for your special day, and in doing so fate made sure I was also close to my grandmother during her final days. I don't think that that was a coincidence.

Deryn, thank you for helping me get the words right, and for helping me get the right words. I love you and will always want room for the way our writer brains talk to each other.

Maureen, thank you for being an ear and a soul to hear about my latest creative endeavor or idea, and for always making my dreams feel rational. I'm so lucky to have a friend and mentor that understands me the way that you do.

Mom, thank you for supporting me even when you don't fully relate to me. I know you are always in my corner, and I will always be in yours.

To the rest of my family, thank you for hopefully honoring my truth and the ways that you inspired these pieces. This book wouldn't be here without our stories to tell.

And of course, thank you one last time to the grandmothers that helped me write this book.

We miss you, we love you, we miss you, we love you.

www.ingramcontent.com/pod-product-compliance
Lightning Source LLC
Chambersburg PA
CBHW071223070526
44584CB00019B/3138